Leptodea leptodon
(Scaleshell Mussel)
Rangewide Status Assessment
1998

Written by: Jennifer Szymanski
U.S. Fish & Wildlife Service
1 Federal Drive
Fort Snelling, Minnesota 55111

Acknowledgments: Numerous State and Federal agency personnel and interested individuals provided information regarding L. leptodon's status. The following individuals graciously provided critical input and review on portions of the manuscript: Bob Anderson, Sue Bruenderman, Al Buchanan, Cindy Chaffee, Kevin Cummings, John Harris, Andy Roberts, and Caryn Vaughn.

Cover: Leptodea leptodon photograph provided by Kevin Cummings.

LEPTODEA LEPTODON STATUS ASSESSMENT

Taxonomy and Physical Description

Leptodea leptodon was described by Rafinesque in 1820. Synonymy includes *Unio velum* (Say 1829), *Sympnynota tenuissima* (Lea 1829), *Lampsilis blatchleyi* (Daniels 1902), and *Lampsilis leptodon* (Rafinesque 1820). *Leptodea leptodon* is commonly known as scaleshell.

A description of the species was provided by Buchanan (1980), Cummings and Mayer (1992), Oesch (1984), and Watters (1995). The shell is typically one to four inches, elongate, and very thin and compressed. The anterior end is rounded; the posterior end in males is bluntly pointed. In females, the periostracum forms a wavy, fluted extension of the shell posteriorly. The dorsal margin is straight; the ventral margin is gently rounded. Umbos are small and low, about even with the hinge line. The beak sculpture is compressed and inconspicuous and consists of four or five double-looped ridges. The periostracum is smooth, yellowish green or brown, with numerous faint green rays. The pseudocardinal teeth are reduced to a small thickened ridge. The lateral teeth are moderately long; two long, indistinct lateral teeth occur in the left valve, one fine tooth in the right. The beak cavity is very shallow or absent. The nacre is pinkish white or light purple and highly iridescent.

Distribution

Leptodea leptodon historically occurred throughout most of the eastern United States. Williams et al. (1993) reported the historical range as Alabama, Arkansas, Illinois, Indiana, Iowa, Kentucky, Michigan, Mississippi, Missouri, Ohio, Oklahoma, South Dakota, Tennessee, and Wisconsin. *Leptodea leptodon* occurrence is also reported from the Minnesota River, Minnesota (Clarke 1996). Gordon (1991), in describing *L. leptodon's* distribution, included a portion of the St. Lawrence drainage. However, the specimens that were the source of the St. Lawrence River record were later identified as wingless examples of *L. fragilis*, which are often seen in New York (David Strayer, Institute of Ecosystem Studies, *in litt.* 1995). Given this and that no other authentic specimens have been found (David Stansbery, Ohio State University, *in litt.* 1995), the historical occurrence of *L. leptodon* in St. Lawrence Basin is doubtful. Similarly, *L. leptodon* occurrence has not been documented in Michigan and Mississippi. Currently, the species is known from a few scattered populations within the Mississippi River System in Missouri, Oklahoma, and Arkansas (Figure 1).

Population Trends

Historically, *L. leptodon* was broadly distributed but locally rare (Gordon 1991, Oesch 1984, Call 1900). Within the last 50 years, it has become increasingly rare and range restricted. Species that persist at low abundances are difficult to census; thus, deriving population trend is nearly impossible. However, reliable inferences can be made based on small population biology theory and observations from field investigations. First, population stability implies, at a minimum, that recruitment exceeds mortality. The presence of juveniles serves as evidence for recruitment. Rangewide surveys have failed to locate juvenile *L. leptodon* specimens in all rivers except for the Meramec River Basin. Second, small populations are more susceptible to extinction due to chance events. All known *L. leptodon* populations, except for populations within the Meramec River Basin, are based on the collection of a few individuals and often only a single specimen. Third, small populations must rely on movement among populations to remain genetically viable. Existing *L. leptodon* occurrences, with the possible exception of those in the Meramec River, are isolated from each other with very little potential for dispersal among them. The lack of evidence for recruitment, the vulnerability of *L. leptodon* populations to chance events, and the isolation of sites, strongly suggests that the *L. leptodon* throughout its range is declining.

To facilitate population comparisons across state lines, criteria for status and trend categories were devised (Appendix 1 & Table 1). Based on these criteria, 13 of 53 known historical populations persist today, i.e., have extant status (Table 2). Of these extant populations, three are likely stable, two are declining, four are presumed declining, and four have unknown trend. An additional six populations may also persist but their current status is uncertain due to lack of recent collections or surveys. The population status for five of these occurrences is likely extirpated and for the other the status is unknown (Table 2).

<u>Upper Mississippi River System</u>- *Leptodea leptodon* is documented from eight rivers and tributaries within this river system (Table 3). However, *L. leptodon* has not been found in more than 50 years and is believed extirpated from the Upper Mississippi River system (Kevin Cummings, Illinois Natural History Survey, *in litt.* 1994).

<u>Middle Mississippi River System</u>- Historically, *L. leptodon* occurred in 25 rivers and tributaries within this system (Table 3). Currently, the species is extant in four, possibly five, rivers within the Meramec River and Missouri River drainages. Of the five populations, two are likely stable, two are presumed declining, and one has unknown population trend (Table 2).

Ohio River Drainage- The species has been extirpated from the entire Ohio River system. The most recent collection date from the Ohio River Basin is 1964 (from Green River, Wayne Davis, Kentucky Dept. of Fish and Wildlife, *in litt.* 1994). All other records are pre-1950 (Cummings; Catherine Gremillion-Smith, Indiana Dept. of Fish and Wildlife; Ron Cicerello, Kentucky Dept. of Fish and Wildlife, *in litt.* 1994; Paul Parmelee, University of Tennessee, pers. comm. 1995)

Meramec River Drainage- During a 1979 survey of the Meramec River Basin, 198 sites were searched and 14 sites had evidence of past or current *L. leptodon* presence (Buchanan 1980). Ten of the sites had evidence (i.e., live or a freshdead shell) of *L. leptodon* persistence. Seven of the 14 sites were in the lower 112 miles of the Meramec River, five in the lower 54 miles of the Bourbeuse River, and two in the lower 10 miles of the Big River. In addition to being restricted to only three rivers, *L. leptodon* is also locally rare. Buchanan found that the species comprised less than 0.1 percent of the living naiades (with live specimens collected at four sites--three in the

2

Meramec and one in the Bourbeuse) found in the Meramec River Basin. The Meramec River, according to Buchanan, supports more freshwater mussel species (42 species) than any other stream in the Meramec River basin. Although the lower 108 miles of the river had suitable habitat for a number of rare species, only the lower 40 miles harbored live *L. leptodon* specimens (Buchanan 1980). Both the Bourbeuse and Big rivers (especially the Big River) had lower species diversity and less suitable habitat than the Meramec River. Suitable habitat was restricted to the lower 54 miles of the Bourbeuse River and lower 10 miles of the Big River (Buchanan 1980). The lower species diversity and abundance of the Big River is attributed to the effects of lead mining. Specifically, from 1978 and beyond, 81,000 cubic yards of mine tailing were discharged into the Big River. As a result, 25 miles of stream was covered and the lower 80 miles of the river were negatively impacted (Alan Buchanan, Missouri Dept. of Conservation, *in litt.* 1995).

An intensive resurvey of the Meramec River Basin occurred in 1997 (Sue Bruenderman, MDOC, *in litt.* 1998). Similar to Buchanan's findings, *L. leptodon* represented only 0.4 percent of the living freshwater mussels, with specimens collected from the Meramec River proper (n=34 at 9 sites, comprising 20.9% of the sites surveyed), the Bourbeuse River (n=10 at 5 sites comprising 19.2% of the sites surveyed), and the Big River (n=2 at 1 site comprising 16.7% of the sites surveyed). *Leptodea leptodon* presence was documented at four of the five sites where Buchanan had collected specimens on the Meramec River (Andy Roberts pers. comm. 1998). The site where *L. leptodon* occurrence was not reconfirmed contained only two live specimens of any mussel species--Buchanan found 93 living individuals. This site no longer supports suitable mussel habitat. Portions of the Meramec River continue to provide suitable habitat, although above river mile 64, mussel species diversity and abundance declines noticeably. The Bourbeuse River has undergone the greatest change with respect to mussel populations. This is especially patent in the lower river. Buchanan found this part of the Bourbouese River to be the most diverse stretch but the 1997 survey found that the mussel populations were decimated. The sites resurveyed in the Big River, which has been the river most affected by past pollution spills, have changed little since the early 1980s. *Leptodea leptodon* specimens were collected from a single, new site. The mussel diversity in the upper portion of the river, as also observed for both the Meramec and Bourbeuse rivers, appears to be declining.

Although the number of *L. leptodon* specimens collected in 1997 is greater than that reported by Buchanan's study, this is not proof of an increasing population. Deriving population trend from a comparison of the studies is difficult because of the low population densities encountered. However, the persistence of *L. leptodon* indicates (because the species is short-lived and thin-shelled) recent recruitment has occurred, although it is unknown whether this recruitment is sufficient to sustain continued survival. Nonetheless, the small number of specimens collected, especially from the Bourbeuse and Big rivers, indicate that the long-term viability of these populations is tenuous. Moreover, the limited mussel habitat available and the loss of mussel beds since 1980 as a result of sedimentation, extreme enrichment and unstable substrates (Buchanan *in litt.* 1997; Roberts pers. comm. 1998) indicate that *L. leptodon* populations within the Meramec River basin are threatened.

Missouri River Drainage- Within the Missouri River drainage, *L. leptodon* is reported from Missouri, Gasconade, Big Piney and South Grand rivers and Auxvasse Creek (Buchanan 1980, 1994; Oesch 1984). *Leptodea leptodon* was last collected from Auxvasse Creek in the late 1960s (Buchanan, *in litt.* 1997). Similarly, the last known collection date for the South Grand is the early 1970s, and this collection site is now inundated by Truman Lake and is unsuitable for *L. leptodon* inhabitance (Buchanan, *in litt.* 1997). The only specimen reported from the Missouri River proper is from South Dakota very close to the Nebraska border (Hoke 1983). This occurrence represents the westernmost record within the Upper Mississippi River system. A subsequent survey failed to relocate live specimens or relict shells (Clarke 1996). A single, fresh dead specimen was collected from Big Piney River in 1981(Bruenderman, *in litt.* 1998). No other information is available on *L. leptodon's* occurrence in this river.

The Gasconade River was surveyed in 1994 and was found to support 36 species of freshwater mussels (Buchanan 1994). *Leptodea leptodon* specimens were collected at eight sites between river miles 6 and 57.7. At two sites only dead shells were found and the remaining six sites had a total of eight live specimens. Overall, *L. leptodon* comprised less than 0.1% of the mussels collected. Several areas of the river were highly unstable, most likely a result of row-crop farming near the bank in conjunction with the 1993 flood. These areas had high cut mud banks with fallen trees into the river, unstable substrate, and contained very few mussels. Many of these areas will, within the next five years, continue to degrade and the mussel fauna will be further impacted with some species possibly disappearing (Buchanan 1994). Below river mile 6, only one stable bar contained a diverse mussel fauna. High silt deposition from Missouri River limits the potential for additional freshwater mussel habitat below this area. If populations still exist in any of the rivers within the Missouri River drainage, their longterm persistence is undoubtably precarious.

Lower Mississippi River System- *Leptodea leptodon* is documented from 20 rivers and tributaries (Table 3). Nine rivers, and possibly an additional five, support *L. leptodon* populations today. Of the fourteen populations, one is likely stable, four are declining, four are presumed declining, and for the remaining five population trend is unknown (Table 2).

St. Francis River- Several mussel surveys have been conducted in portions and throughout the length of the St. Francis River (Bates and Dennis 1983, Ahlstedt and Jenkinson 1987, Clarke 1985, Harris 1986, Rust 1993). Records of dead mussels and relic shells indicate that at one time mussels were distributed throughout the river (Bates and Dennis 1983). *Leptodea leptodon* occurrence is documented at two sites by single specimens (Clarke 1985). Much of the St. Francis River from the mouth above Helena, Arkansas to Wappapello Dam, Missouri has been drastically altered by channelization, construction of levees, diversion ditches, and control structures and floodways (Ahlstedt and Jenkinson 1987, Bates and Dennis 1983). Bates and Dennis (1983) found that of the 54 sites sampled, 15 were productive, 10 marginal, and 29 had either no shells or dead specimens only. Although *L. leptodon* was not collected, they noted that three areas, comprising 48 miles, provided suitable mussel habitat: Wappapello Dam, MO to Mingo Ditch, MO; Parkin, AR to Madison, AR; and Marianna to the confluence with the Mississippi River at Helena, AR. The remaining river miles are unsuitable for mussel habitation.

If *L. leptodon* is extant, it occurs in very small numbers and is confined to the remaining suitable patches.

White River Drainage- *Leptodea leptodon* is documented from White River proper, James River,-Spring River, South Fork Spring, Strawberry River, Myatt Creek, and Middle Fork Little Red River. The sole White River specimen was collected in 1902 near Garfield, Arkansas (Clarke 1996). A late 1970s survey of the White River between Beaver Reservoir and its headwaters failed to relocate live or dead *L. leptodon* individuals (Gordon 1980). Municipal pollution, gravel dredging, and dam construction have rendered this reach of the river unsuitable for mussels. Bates and Dennis (1983) surveyed the White River from Newport, AR to the confluence of the Mississippi River. In their report, they concluded that navigational maintenance activities continue to destroy habitat. As a result, mussel populations have been relegated to a few refugial sites, none of which support *L. leptodon*. Specimens have not been collected from the James River, a tributary of the White River, since before 1950 (Clarke 1996). It is unlikely that either river currently supports *L. leptodon*.

An eight-mile section of the Spring River supports a diverse assemblage of freshwater mussels (Gordon et al. 1979 and 1984, Arkansas Highway and Transportation Dept 1984, Miller and Hartfield 1986). Eight specimens of *L. leptodon* have been collected from this river (Cummings *in litt* 1994, Clarke 1996, Arkansas State Hwy. and Transportation Dept. 1984, Miller and Nelson 1984). A 1984 (Gordon et al. 1984) survey found suitable mussel habitat between river miles 3.2 and 11.0, although species richness below river mile 9 (at the confluence of Eleven Point River) declined markedly. Gordon and colleagues (1984), as well as Miller and Hartfield (1986), reported that the lower three miles of river were completely depauperate of mussels and contained no suitable habitat (Miller and Hartfield 1986, Gordon et al. 1984). Sand and gravel dredging, cattle wading, siltation, and surface run-off of pesticide and fertilizer appear to be contributing factors in the degradation of this river reach (Gordon et al. 1984). A 1993 survey of Spring River failed to document *L. leptodon* presence (John Harris, Arkansas State University, *in litt.* 1997).

Leptodea leptodon was collected from the South Fork Spring River in 1983 and 1990. During the 1983 survey (Harris *in litt.* 1997), four specimens near Saddle, Arkansas and one specimen and one valve north of Hunt, Arkansas were collected. During a subsequent visit in 1990 (Harris pers. comm. 1995) fairly young adults were collected. Although juveniles were not found, the presence of young adults signifies that reproduction has occurred in recent years. South Fork Spring and Meramec rivers appear to support the most robust *L. leptodon* populations.

The Strawberry River and the Myatt Creek occurrences are single specimen collections (Harris *in litt* 1997). The Strawberry River specimen (collected live in 1996) was collected near the confluence with Clayton Creek in Lawrence County. A single relict specimen was collected in 1996 from Myatt Creek in Fulton County (Harris *in litt* 1997).

The historical locality (near Shirley, Van Buren County, Arkansas) of the single, known specimen from the Middle Fork of the Little Red River no longer supports mussel habitat. According to

Clarke (1987), suitable mussel habitat exists for a six-mile stretch from the confluence of Tick Creek upstream to the mouth of Meadow Creek. Below Tick Creek, only dead mussels were found. Upstream of Meadow Creek, the river recedes to form a series of isolated pools during dry summer months.

Arkansas River Drainage- *Leptodea leptodon* has been collected from the Arkansas River system in Oklahoma and Arkansas. The species is reported from the Poteau River in Oklahoma (Gordon 1991), Frog Bayou in Arkansas (Harris and Gordon 1987), the South Fourche La Fave and Mulberry rivers in Arkansas (Gordon 1991 and Harris 1992). Despite several freshwater mussel surveys of the Poteau River (Isely 1925, White 1977*in* Harris 1994, Branson 1984, and Harris 1994), only a single, undated specimen has been collected (Gordon 1980). *Leptodea leptodon* persistent in Poteau River is doubtful.

Leptodea leptodon is documented from the Frog Bayou by two specimens (Gordon 1980). One of the specimens was collected at a site that is now inundated by the Beaver Reservoir. The most recent collection was a fresh dead individual, accompanied by several other fresh dead mussel species, during a 1979 survey (Gordon 1980). Gordon noted that this site and other nearby sites were recently disturbed by streambank bulldozing upstream. He also reported in-stream gravel mining activities at several sites. Within Frog Bayou, potential habitat is restricted to the area between Rudy and the confluence of the Arkansas River. Above Rudy, the river is impacted by the two reservoirs; one near Maddux Spring and the other at Mountainburg. At the confluence of the Arkansas River, live mussels have not been found--likely due to dredging activities (Gordon 1980). The occurrence of *L. leptodon* is uncertain, but if present the population is in jeopardy due to limited habitat and in-stream mining activities.

The South Fourche La Fave River is dominated by a few widely distributed and abundant species. The only *L. leptodon* record from this river is a single, live specimen found in 1991 (Harris 1992). The potential of additional mussels populations is unlikely due to the limited availability of suitable substrate. Similarly, other major tributaries of the South Fourche La Fave River provide little opportunity for mussel occurrence. Similar to the Frog Bayou, persistence of *L. leptodon* in this river is in doubt.

Although Gordon (1991) indicated *L. leptodon* occurrence in the Mulberry River, documentation is lacking (i.e., no written acknowledgment). A recent survey failed to obtain evidence of *L. leptodon* presence as well (Craig Hilborne, U.S. Forest Service, pers. comm. 1995; Stoeckel et al. 1995). *Leptodea leptodon* existence in the Mulberry River is unlikely.

Red River Drainage- The historical distribution of *L. leptodon* in the Red River drainage includes Kiamichi River (OK), Gates Creek (OK), Little River (OK and AR), Mountian Fork (OK), Cossatot River (AR), Saline River (AR), and Ouachita River (AR).

A single, undated specimen was collected from Gates Creek, a tributary of the Kiamichi River (Valentine and Stansbery 1971). The first collection date from the Kiamichi River is 1925 (Isley

1925). From Isley's work, it is obvious that the Kiamichi River supported a diverse and abundant mussel fauna. He collected 36 specimens of *L. leptodon* at one of 22 stations visited. As recently as 1987 (Clarke 1987), the Kiamichi River was described as "in remarkably good condition" and a "faunal treasure". However, despite extensive searches of the Kiamichi River over the last 11 years, only a single fresh dead shell (in 1987) has been collected (CarynVaughn, Oklahoma Biological Survey, pers. comm. 1997; Charles Mather, University of Science and Arts of Oklahoma, *in litt.* 1984 and 1995). Vaughn (pers. comm. 1997) failed to find even a *L. leptodon* shell during three years (1993-1996) of surveys in the Red River system. However, the Kiamichi River is in relatively good shape above the Hugo Reservoir, (Clarke 1987) and may still support a remnant population of *L. leptodon.* A potential threat to the Kiamichi River is a proposed reservoir at Tuskahoma (located above Hugo Reservoir). Although the U.S. Army Corps of Engineers has authorized construction, the lack of a local sponsor has rendered the project "inactive" (Martinez, pers comm. 1997). If constructed, the devastating effects associated with reservoirs (e.g., increased siltation and altered temperature regime) are likely to destroy the diverse mussel fauna that currently inhabits the Kiamichi River.

Unlike the Kiamichi River, the Little River continues to be greatly affected by sewage pollution, gravel dredging, and reservoir effects. The mainstem of the river is impounded by the Pine Creek Reservoir. Further downstream, a major tributary to the Little River, the Mountain Fork River, is impounded by Broken Bow Reservoir. Although lacking evidence of *L. leptodon* persistence, the Little River above the Pine Creek Reservoir supports healthy mussel populations (Vaughn *in litt.* 1997). Below Pine Creek Lake, the mussel fauna is severely depleted but recovers with increasing distance from the impoundment (Vaughn *in litt.*1997). A *L. leptodon* specimen was reported from Mountain Fork by Valentine and Stansbery (1971). Clarke (1987) believed that, based on the presence of mussel populations at the confluence of Mountain Fork and beyond the Arkansas border, damage to Mountain Fork from the Broken Bow Reservoir has not occurred. However, Vaughn (*in litt.* 1997) indicated that these populations are now severely depleted with most no longer containing live mussels. Although extensive surveys throughout the length of Little River failed to collect *L. leptodon*, suitable habitat remains and *L. leptodon* individuals may persist (Vaughn *in litt.* 1997). If *L. leptodon* does not occur there now, however, discharge of hypolimnectic water from Pine Creek and periodic discharge of pollution from Rolling Fork Creek prevents future recolonization (Clarke 1987).

If *L. leptodon* still occurs in the Red River drainage in Oklahoma, extant populations are small and are likely restricted to the few remaining, isolated suitable areas in the Kiamichi and Mt. Fork rivers. Given the extensive survey effort over the last decade, *L. leptodon* long-term persistence in Oklahoma is tenuous.

The occurrence of *L. Leptodon* in the Cossatot and Saline rivers is attributed to single specimens collected in 1983 (Harris *in litt.* 1997) and 1987 (Harris pers. comm. 1995), respectively. No other information is available for either river. *Leptodea leptodon* occurrence in the Ouachita River and its two tributaries, the Saline River and Little Missouri River, is sporadic as well. Both the Little Missouri and Saline rivers records are from single specimens. The Saline River specimen was collected in 1946 (Clarke 1996), and the Little Missouri River collection record is from 1995 (Harris *in litt.* 1997). *Leptodea leptodon* occurrence in the Ouachita River is documented by four undated museum specimens from Arkadelphia, Clark County, Arkansas (Clarke 1996). Ouachita River has been severely impacted by hydroelectric dams and artificial lakes. The "Old River," an oxbow system off the mainstem, is now essentially a series of muddy, stagnant pools with water quality problems resulting from dumps, interspersed with small, isolated pockets of suitable mussel habitat (Clarke 1987). Based on the small number of collections and the limited habitat available, the long-term persistence in Cossatot, Saline, Little Missouri, and Ouachita rivers is precarious.

Habitat

Although always somewhat rare, *L. leptodon* apparently was not habitat limited. According to published accounts, the species occupied a wide variety of habitat types. For example, Buchanan (1980, 1994) and Gordon (1991) reported *L. leptodon* from riffle areas with substrate assemblages of gravel, cobble, boulder, and occasionally mud or sand. Oesch (1984) considered *L. leptodon* a typical riffle species, occurring only in clear, unpolluted water with good current. Conversely, Call (1900), Goodrich and Van der Schalie (1944), and Cummings and Mayer (1992) reported collections from muddy bottoms of big rivers. The unifying characteristic appears to be an intact system with good water quality. This is consistent with the current distribution of *L. leptodon*. Most extant populations are restricted to river stretches that support a high diversity of freshwater mussels (Buchanan 1980, Harris 1992) and that have maintained relatively good water quality.

Ecology

Very little is known about the ecology of *L. leptodon* specifically. Baker (1928 in Buchanan 1980 and Oesch 1984) surmised that the breeding season is bradytictic (i.e., long-term breeder with larvae held until the following spring or summer). This was based on reports of glochidia present in the ectobranchous marsupia in September, October, November, and March (Gordon 1991). Watters (1995) provides a overview of the unionid life cycle. The female stores the unfertilized eggs in a region of the gills called marsupia. She takes up sperm liberated into the water by the male. Over a period of days to months, the fertilized eggs develop into glochidia (i.e., larvae). The female expels glochidia into the water which then attach to suitable hosts. Host fish specificity is seemingly the rule rather than the exception for most of the mussel species (Neves 1993). Following proper infestation, glochidia transform into juveniles and excyst. The length of time is dependent on water temperature. For further information on the life history of freshwater mussels, see Gordon and Layzer (1989) and Watters (1995).

Threats

A. Present or threatened destruction, modification, or curtailment of habitat or range: The loss of mussel diversity in the U.S. has been well documented and is a major concern for conservation biologists. In a review of the conservation status of native freshwater fauna, the American Fisheries Society found that of the 297 native freshwater mussels, 71 percent are imperiled (Williams et al. 1993). Similarly, The Nature Conservancy recognizes 55 percent of North America's mussel fauna as extinct or imperiled (Master 1990 *in* Williams et al. 1993). The current status of *L. leptodon* exemplifies the loss of mussel diversity. The range of *L. leptodon* was once expansive, spanning the Mississippi River Basin in at least 53 rivers and 13 States. Today, the range is significantly reduced with known extant populations persisting in only 13 rivers in three States.

Arguably, *L. leptodon* has suffered a greater range restriction than any other unionid. *Leptodea leptodon* has been decimated from the entire Upper and most of the Middle Mississippi River drainages. Much of the decline occurred before mid-century; having been last documented from Alabama, Illinois, Indiana, Iowa, Kentucky, Ohio, Tennessee, and Wisconsin more than 30, and for most more than 50, years ago (Thomas Watters, Ohio State University, *in litt.* 1995; Parmelee and David Heath, Wisconsin Department of Natural Resources, pers. comm. 1995; Cummings, Smith, and Cicerello, *in litt.* 1994; Michael Hoggarth, Otterbein College and Patricia Jones, Ohio Dept. of Natural Resources, *in litt.* 1994; Stansbery 1976). As with most endangered mussels, the principal cause of this decline is habitat destruction. Habitat degradation--as a result of physical, chemical, and biological alteration--has and continues to threaten *L. leptodon* populations. The major causes of such alteration are channelization, damming and impoundment, and nonpoint and point source pollution. The most pernicious effects of these factors are contamination and sedimentation (Fuller 1974, Myers et al. 1985, USSCS 1988). Freshwater mussels, because of their sedentary nature and their filter-feeding habit, are very susceptible to degraded water quality. Reports of wholesale destruction of mussel populations as a consequence of pollution and sedimentation date back to the late 19th and early 20th centuries (Lewis 1868, Ortmann 1909 *in* Fuller 1974), and continue to be implicated as the primary factors in the loss of mussel diversity (Vaughn 1993, Goudreau et al. 1988; Coon et al. 1977).

Contamination

Contamination of waterways is a result of point and nonpoint source pollution. Point source pollution refers to entry of material from a discrete, identifiable source (e.g., industrial effluents, sewage treatment plants, solid waste disposal sites). Little information exists on the specific toxicity of contaminants to mussels. However, freshwater mussel mortality from toxic spills and chronic lethality of polluted water are well documented (Lewis 1868 *in* Neves 1993, Ortmann 1909, and Baker 1928 *in* Fuller 1974; Cairns et al. 1971 *in* Neves 1993; Goudreau et al. 1988). It is generally accepted that contaminants are at least partially responsible for decreases in population densities, ranges, and diversity of unionids. Decline and elimination of populations may be due to acute and chronic toxic effects that result in direct mortality, reduced reproductive success, or compromised health of the animal or host fish. Mussels, as filter-feeders, are exposed to contaminants that dissolve in water and deposit in bottom substrate. The toxicity of pollutants stored in mussel tissue can greatly exceed the levels found in surrounding water, i.e., bioaccumulate (USFWS in prep.). Furthermore, sediment and dissolved organic matter act

9

synergistically with metallic pollution (USFWS in prep). As toxic metals are adsorbed onto suspended particles (Tessier and Campbell 1987 *in* USFWS in prep.), they can accumulate and directly affect filter-feeding animals (USFWS in prep.). This can lead to shell calcification interference (Rosenberg and Henschen 1986). The sedentary nature of mussels predisposes *L. leptodon* to chronic water quality problems. Although adult mussels are able to close their valves for an extended period of time to avoid acute toxic effects (Holwerda and Veenhof 1984), this mechanism is not effective for chronic toxic exposure (Neves 1993). Research indicates that glochidia and juveniles are more sensitive to toxicants than adults (Goudreau et al. 1993, Neves 1993); yet the larval stage lacks valve closure capabilities. Thus, larvae are vulnerable to both acute and chronic toxic effects.

Nonpoint source pollution is responsible for more than half of all water pollution (Chesters and Schierow 1985). This type of pollution refers to entry of material into the environment from a diffuse source. The major contributors of nonpoint source pollution include agricultural, urban, construction, and silvicultural activities (Myers et al. 1985). The most pervasive source of nonpoint contamination is agricultural operations (Thomas 1985). Fertilizers, manure and pesticides are the primary derivations of these pollutants, which can be transported with sediment (adsorbed pollutants) or in solution (soluble pollutants). Nitrogen and phosphorus are the major pollutants associated with water quality degradation (Myers et al. 1985). These pollutants accelerate eutrophication (i.e., organic enrichment) of water bodies (Fuller 1974). Freshwater mussels are considered one of the most sensitive faunal groups to organic enrichment (Goudreau et al. 1988). Although organic enrichment can be beneficial (i.e., increase in food production), it can also be destructive through smothering and chemical alteration (Dance 1981*in* Wolcott and Neves 1990). Organic enrichment increases aquatic plant productivity, which correlates to an increase in decaying organic matter. As a result, oxygen is depleted, current slackens, carbon dioxide production increases, and pH decreases--all of which are inimical to the survival of most freshwater mussels (Fuller 1974).

Additionally, high concentrations of phosphorus, potassium, ammonium, bacteria, and organic matter in manure can contaminate surface waters when animals are allowed direct access to streams (Chesters and Schierow 1985, Myers et al. 1985) or when animal wastes are not properly stored. In addition to causing organic enrichment, phosphorus can also hinder shell development (Rosenberg and Henschen 1986 *in* Goudreau et al. 1988). Potassium at high concentrations can be toxic to mussels and can be responsible for the loss of entire populations (Fuller 1974). Ammonia has both lethal and sublethal effects. Toxic ammonia induces glochidial closure and thus interferes with fish host infection (Goudreau et al. 1988). Pollutants from fertilizers applied around homes, golf courses, and parks may also add to the degradation of water quality (Myers et al. 1985). Likewise, construction sites can significantly degrade waterbodies. These areas generate pollutants, including fertilizers, pesticides, petroleum products, and a variety of other construction materials, that degrade water quality and are toxic to aquatic organisms (Myers et al. 1985).

Sedimentation

Sediment is material that is in suspension, is being transported, or has been moved as the result of erosion (USSCS 1988). The water quality impacts caused by sedimentation are numerous. In general, it affects aquatic biota by altering the substratum (Ellis 1936, USSCS 1988, Myers et al. 1985) and by altering the chemical and physical composition of the water (Ellis 1936, Myers et al. 1985, USSCS 1988). Sedimentation directly affects freshwater mussel survival by interfering with respiration and feeding. Having great difficulty in escaping smothering conditions (Imlay 1972), a sudden or slow blanketing of stream bottom with sediment can suffocate freshwater mussels (Ellis 1936). Increased sediment levels may also cause reduced feeding efficiency-- empirical studies have found that mussels remain close 25-40 percent longer when exposed to greater sedimentation concentrations than under normal conditions (Ellis 1936)--which can lead to decreased growth and survival (Bayne et al. 1981 *in* Spacie and Chaney 1993).

Sedimentation also influences the physical and chemical composition of the water. Suspended materials are very effective in limiting light penetration through the water column which reduces the production of phytoplankton (a food source for mussels) and alters the water temperature. Extreme fluctuations in water temperature can have lethal effects (Ray 1977 *in* Imlay 1982). Decreases in temperature may induce egg mass abortion (with sudden decreases in temperature; Matteson 1948 *in* Fuller 1974) and decrease reproductive success by dulling glochidial response to opportunities for host fish infection (Arey 1921 *in* Fuller 1974). Conversely, increasing temperature can result in increased oxygen demand, shorten excystment period (Young 1911 *in* Fuller 1974), and increase toxic ammonia concentrations (Goudreau et al. 1988). Sedimentation also causes retention of organic material and other substances. This alters the oxygen demand and the pH of the water, and increases bacterial concentrations (Ellis 1936). Low levels of dissolved oxygen impair mussel growth (Imlay and Paige 1972). Decreases in pH can induce closure (Matteson 1955 *in* Fuller 1974) and permit suspended materials to remain in suspension, both of which can interfere with mussel feeding activities (Fuller 1974). Moreover, when sediment settles out of suspension, it may carry with it adsorbed organic materials. This can result in increased and localized enrichment of the stream (Fuller 1974), which as previously discussed can have adverse effects. In addition, pollutants stored in the soil can be carried by the sediment (Myers et al. 1985). Thus, increased sediment loads can also facilitate contamination of water bodies.

Although sedimentation is a natural process, agricultural encroachment, channelization and damming, timber harvesting within riparian zones, heavy recreational use, urbanization, as well as other landuse activities greatly accelerate erosion (Waters 1995, Myers et al. 1985, Chesters and Schierow 1985). Agriculture is the primary source of sedimentation (Myers et al. 1985; USEPA 1990 *in* Waters 1995). This is not surprising given that more than half of all non-federal land is used for agricultural purposes (based on a 1985 estimate, Myers et al. 1985). It has been long recognized that adjacent landuse influences the stream sediment load and discharge (Waters 1995; Myers et al. 1985; Sorensen et al. 1977). Striffler (1964 *in* Waters 1995) reported that streams within forested or other well-vegetated idle land had stable flows and less sediment; whereas, streams in cultivated or pastured watersheds had heavy sediment and variable flows.

Channelization and damming are also major sources of sedimentation. Channelization and other dredging operations (e.g., sand and gravel mining) can bury, crush, or physically remove mussels with the substrate (Watters 1995). It also causes loss of substrate stability (Hartfield 1993), which results in the release of sediment and pollutants. In some instances, the mussel fauna and habitat are severely diminished as documented in the Yellow and Kankakee rivers in Indiana, the Big Vermillion River in Illinois, and the Ohio River (Fuller 1974). Dams have similar effects by creating sediment traps upstream and powerful currents below. Resultant currents move sediment over beds and smother mussels and erode streambanks (Fuller 1974). Impoundments also increase sediment load by decreasing the water's sediment carrying capacity (Bates 1962, Negus 1966 in Watters 1995). Beyond sedimentation impacts, impoundments affect downstream mussel populations by inducing scouring, changing temperature regimes, and altering habitat, food, and fish host availability (Vaughn, in litt. 1997). Scour is a major cause of mussel mortality below dams (Layzer et al. 1993). Most detrimental, however, is the disruption of reproductive processes (Fuller 1974). Impoundments, which interfere with fish movement, alter normal fish behavior, reduce the amount of suitable substrate, and diminish recruitment success (Vaughn 1993). Layzer and colleagues (1993) found that the cold water releases associated with some impoundments led to a 30 to 60 percent decrease of the mussel fauna. Other sublethal effects include reduced growth and increased eutrophication (Watters 1995).

Urbanization and silvicultural activities are important contributors of sedimentation as well. Construction, although representing a small fraction of the nationwide sediment load in receiving waters, can have enormous, immediate impacts. Soil erosion rates are typically 10 to 20 times those on agricultural land and run-off rates may be 100 times greater (Myers et al. 1985). Over short periods of time, construction activities can contribute more sediment to streams than was previously deposited over several decades. Likewise, silviculture operations, such as road building and harvesting operations, can also generate substantial amounts of sediment (Myers et al. 1985). Moreover, deforestation causes irregular stream flow, high water temperatures, and lowered dissolved oxygen--all which can adversely affect freshwater mussel survival for years after the timber harvest (Fuller 1974).

Leptodea leptodon appears to be especially susceptible to contamination and sedimentation. Historically, the species was widespread and occurred in diverse habitat; whereas today, *L. leptodon* no longer occurs at sites which still support other endangered unionids (i.e., at sites which have not been terribly altered). This suggests that *L. leptodon* is especially sensitive to changes that have occurred (e.g., degraded water quality). Given the pervasiveness of the sources of pollution and sedimentation, it is apparent that these threats will continue to be problematic for *L. leptodon*. Nonpoint and point source pollution is currently affecting the Spring River in Arkansas (Gordon et al. 1984, Miller and Hartfield 1986) and the Little River in Oklahoma (Clarke 1987, Vaughn 1994). Sedimentation is causing deleterious effects in the Meramec River, MO (Roberts, pers. comm. 1998); Gasconade River, MO (Buchanan 1994); Frog Bayou, AR (Gordon 1980); and Spring River, AR (Gordon et al. 1984). Sand and gravel mining are eliminating important pool habitat (for both *L. leptodon* and potential fish hosts) in the Meramec and Gasconade rivers in Missouri (Bruenderman pers. comm. 1998). Impoundments, channelization, and other dredging activities (e.g., sand and gravel mining) are impairing water quality in Frog Bayou, AR (Gordon 1980); St. Francis River, AR (Ahlstedt and Jenkinson 1987); White River, AR (Bates and Dennis 1983); Spring River, AR (Gordon et al. 1984); and Ouachita River, AR (Clarke 1987). The proposed Kiamichi River reservoir, if constructed, will undoubtably have devastating impacts. Nearly all *L. leptodon* populations are now restricted to small stretches of rivers with little, if any, potential for expansion or recolonization to other areas. The Little River in Oklahoma, for example, is so degraded by sewage pollution, gravel dredging, and reservoir construction that only a few, small stretches are able support mussel populations.

B. Overutilization for scientific or commercial purposes: It is unlikely that *L. leptodon*, because of its small size and thin shell, was ever purposefully collected by commercial musselers. It is plausible, however, that extirpated populations were subjected to over-harvesting activities. For example, according to local fishermen, mussel beds in the Spring and Black rivers were severely over-collected during a period of extended drought and most beds were completely destroyed (Gordon et al. 1984). Thus, *L. leptodon* populations may have been indirectly impacted (e.g., by habitat destruction, removal from the stream, and discarded or improper replacement). Today, incidental collecting could potentially be detrimental to existing populations. In addition to possibly destroying or modifying the stream bed, collection or improper replacement of only a few individuals--given that *L. leptodon* now occurs in very small, isolated populations--could decimate an entire population. Musseling techniques, such as brailling, are nonselective harvesting methods that typically result in unwanted and juvenile individuals being discarded (Williams et al. 1993). Even for those individuals that are returned to the stream, mortality can still occur (Williams et al. 1993). Furthermore, gravid females may abort when disturbed (Imlay 1972), resulting in a loss of an individual's entire reproductive effort.

C. Disease or predation: Although natural predation is not problematic for stable, healthy populations, small mammal predation could potentially pose a problem for *L. leptodon* populations (Gordon 1991). The extant *L. leptodon* populations in Arkansas and Oklahoma are small, isolated and have very limited recolonization potential. Consequently, predation could exacerbate ongoing population declines.

Bacteria and protozoans persist at unnaturally high concentrations in streams with high sediment load or in waterbodies affected by point source pollution, such as sewage treatment plants (Goudreau et al. 1988). At these densities, ova and glochidia are vulnerable to attack (Ellis 1929 *in* Fuller 1974) and mussel growth can be slowed (Imlay and Paige 1972).

D. Inadequacy of existing regulatory mechanisms:. The River and Harbors Act of 1899 was the first of a sequence of federal laws to protect surface waters. This Act was promulgated to curb refuse disposal. Although this law has had beneficial effects, the Water Pollution Control Act of 1948 was the first law that explicitly intended to abate water pollution and to assign responsibility to the individual States. Subsequent amendments to the Act in 1956 and 1961 provided construction grants for wastewater treatment plants and provided research funds to study pollution effects and to develop improved methods of effluent treatment. The Wild and Scenic

13

Rivers Act of 1968 provided a mechanism to identify and protect river reaches by prohibition of federal approval or assistance for water projects that would have adverse effects. However, the legislation provided inadequate protection from private development (Neves 1993). The passage of the Clean Water Act of 1972 (CWA) set the stage for the regulations and the water standards that exist today. Goals of the CWA include protection and enhancement of fish, shellfish, and wildlife; providing conditions suitable for recreation in surface waters; and eliminating the discharge of pollutants in U.S. waters.

Although positive consequences (e.g., a decrease in lead and fecal coliform bacteria) have been realized following the passage of these Acts, degraded water quality still presents problems for sensitive aquatic organisms such as freshwater mussels. Specifically, nationwide sampling has indicated increases in nitrate, chloride, arsenic, and cadmium concentrations (Neves 1993). Non-point pollution sources appear to be the cause of increases in nitrogen trend. Agriculture is recognized as the most prominent source of non-point source pollutants, affecting more than two-thirds of the nation's river basins (Neves 1993). However, only a few regulations aimed at controlling runoff have been imposed on the agricultural community. The programs that address nonpoint source pollution are mostly voluntary, and unfortunately contamination and sedimentation continue to threaten freshwater mussel survival.

Although recognized by species experts as threatened in Arkansas, *L. leptodon* is not afforded state protection (Table 4). Missouri and Oklahoma afford State protective status for *L. leptodon*--listed as rare and species of concern, respectively (Bruenderman, *in litt.* 1998; Vaughn pers. comm. 1995). State regulations, however, provide inadequate protection from direct take and habitat destruction (Martinez; McKenzie; pers. comm. 1997). Without habitat protection, neither slowing nor prevention of *L. leptodon* decline will occur.

E. Other manmade or natural factors: As a consequence of the above factors, the inherent biological traits of freshwater mussels increase their vulnerability to extinction (Neves 1993). For example, the larval stage (glochidium) of most mussels is dependent on a few or a specific host fish (Neves 1993). Despite the tremendous fecundity of females, this trait greatly reduces the likelihood of contact between glochidia and suitable hosts. Watters (1995) postulated that the glochidia must acquire suitable hosts within 24 hours. Obviously, reduction or loss of host fish populations will adversely impact *L. leptodon* populations. Once a larva successfully transforms on a host, it is further challenged with dropping off (known as excystment) into suitable habitat. Watters (1995) reported that estimated chances of successful transformation and excystment range from 0.0001% (Jansen and Hanson 1991) and 0.000001% (Young and Williams 1984). As a result of fish host-specificity and the difficulty of locating suitable habitat, freshwater mussel population growth occurs very slowly. Furthermore, the sedentary nature of mussels limits their dispersal capability. This trait coupled with low recruitment success translates into the need for decades of immigration and recruitment for re-establishment of self-sustaining populations. Thus, achieving longterm survival for species that have undergone population decline is an protracted and ardous task. Accomplishing this task, however, is nearly impossible for those species confronted habitat degradation as well.

14

The threats to *L. leptodon* survival posed by the above factors are exacerbated by the small number of low density populations that remain. Although *L. leptodon* was always somewhat rare, the current population densities are likely much lower (due to the previously identified threats) than historical levels. Despite any evolutionary adaptations for rarity, habitat loss and degradation increase a species vulnerability to extinction (Noss and Cooperrider 1994). Numerous studies have shown that with decreasing habitat availability, the probability of extinction increases. Similarly, as the number of occupied sites decreases, the likelihood of extinction increases (Vaughn 1993). This increased vulnerability is the result of chance events. Environmental variation, random or predictable, naturally causes fluctuations in populations. However, populations with small numbers are more likely to fluctuate below the minimum viable population (i.e., the minimum number of individuals needed in a population to survive). If population levels stay below this minimum size, an inevitable, and often irreversible, slide toward extinction will occur. Small populations are also more susceptible to inbreeding depression and genetic drift. Populations subjected to either of these problems usually have low genetic diversity, which reduces fertility and survivorship. Lastly, chance variation in age and sex ratios can affect birth and deaths rates. Skewing of the demographics may lead to death rates exceeding the birth rates, and when this occurs in small populations there is a higher risk of extinction.

Similarly, the fertilization success of mussels may be related to population density, with a threshold density required for any reproductive success to occur (Downing et al. 1993 *in* Watters 1995). Small mussel populations may have individuals too scattered to reproduce effectively (Wilson and Clark 1912 *in* Fuller 1974). Many of the remaining *L. leptodon* populations may be at or below this threshold density. These populations will be, if one of the aforementioned threats go unabated, forced below or forced to remain below the minimum threshold. As a result, the current decline to extinction will be accelerated.

Furthermore, species that occur in low numbers must rely on dispersal and recolonization for long-term persistence. In order to retain genetic viability and guard against chance extinction, movement between local populations must occur (i.e., a functional metapopulation, Appendix 1). Although *L. leptodon* naturally occurs in patches and necessarily possesses mechanisms to adapt to such a population structure, anthropogenic influences have fragmented and furthered lengthened the distance between populations. Empirical studies have shown that with increasing isolation colonization rates decrease. Also as previously explained, natural recolonization of mussels occurs at a very low rate (Vaughn 1993). Therefore, it is imperative for long-term freshwater mussel survival that a metapopulation structure is preserved. Unfortunately, many of the extant *L. leptodon* populations now occur as single, isolated sites. These insular populations are very susceptible to chance events and extinction with no chance of recolonization.

Lastly, the invasion of the exotic zebra mussel (*Dreissena polymorpha*) threatens all native unionids through suffocation and competition for space, food, and survival of glochidia. Currently, the native freshwater mussel fauna of the Mississippi and Ohio rivers is being decimated by the invasion of the zebra mussel (Clarke 1995). The natural history of zebra mussels is not completely understood; therefore, effective control measures are not yet known.

Given that recreational and commercial vessels greatly facilitate zebra mussel movement and because of the proliferation and spread that has occurred, invasion of the *D. polymorpha* into portions of the lower Mississippi River Basin appears inevitable (Buchanan pers. comm. 1995). If zebra mussel invasion does indeed occur, the continued survival of *L. leptodon* will be jeopardized.

Conservation Efforts

Interest in the conservation of freshwater mussels dates back to the turn of the century and is even more evident today. Government agencies, researchers, private organizations, and individuals are working together to preserve North American native mussel fauna. Several of these efforts directly and indirectly benefit *L. leptodon*. First, numerous studies aimed at investigating the ecology (e.g., glochidial infections, habitat preferences, etc.) and efforts to develop management protocols (e.g., monitoring, relocation and reintroduction techniques) for specific mussel species are ongoing. Information garnered from these studies may provide insightful information for *L. leptodon* conservation. Next, the rapid spread of the zebra mussel has precipitated the formation of committees whose sole purposes are to address the zebra mussel control. The Ohio River Zebra Mussel Group has developed a strategic plan that outlines the actions needed for avoidance, minimization, and mitigation. Obviously, any action that thwarts zebra mussel dispersal will aid in the conservation of *L. leptodon*. Finally, The Nature Conservancy has initiated the development and the distribution of species databases which describe what is and is not known for specific taxa. These databases facilitate species management and research. For example, a 1991 TNC abstract was used as a source of distribution records for this assessment. Efforts such as this will provide a forum for researchers, government agencies, and other interested parties to easily and effectively communicate research findings and further conservation needs.

APPENDIX 1 - DEFINITIONS

Population Terminology (Vaughn 1993):
Local population refers to an assemblage of individuals that more or less interact with each other in the course of their routine feeding and breeding activities

Metapopulation or river population refers the species at a regional scale at which individuals infrequently move from one local population to another, typically across unsuitable habitat and with risk of failure to locate another suitable patch

Species or population at the geographic scale refers to the species entire range; individuals typically have no possibility of moving to most parts of its range.

<u>Table Definitions:</u>
*Last Date Collected: Last collection date regardless of condition (live, fresh dead or weathered).

*Status: A qualitative assessment of the <u>current</u> existence of a local population. Due to the low population densities of current *L. leptodon* occurrences, ascertaining existence is difficult. Thus, status is assigned based on the following criteria.

> Extant (E) status is assigned if at least one live or fresh dead specimen has been collected since 1980, **and** no evidence of significant habitat destruction since last date of collection.

> Likely Extirpated (LX) status (i.e., could be extant but likely extirpated) is assigned if live or fresh dead specimens have not been collected since 1980 despite subsequent surveys but suitable habitat patches remain.

> Extirpated (X) status is assigned if: (1) thorough post 1980 surveys have failed to find any evidence of *L. leptodon*'s occurrence; **or** (2)virtually all suitable habitat has been eliminated; **or** (3) last date of collection was before 1967.

> Unknown (UK) status is assigned if: (1) specimens not collected since 1980 <u>and</u> no other information is available; **or** (2) post 1980 surveys lacking but suitable habitat patches remain.

*Trend: A qualitative assessment of change in a local population's numbers and its future condition. Although ascertaining population trend is difficult, inferences are made based on number and age of specimens collected, date of last collection, habitat availability, and threats.

> Stable (S) trend (i.e, longterm persistence is probable) is assigned if post 1980 collections of juveniles or young adults (i.e., less than 2 years of age), **and** optimal habitat is available, **and** no evidence of immediate threats to habitat.

> Likely Stable (LS) trend (i.e., longterm persistence is possible but unsure) was assigned if: (1) post-1980 collections of relatively young adults <u>and</u> good habitat is available; **or** (2) post 1980 surveys with only mature live or fresh dead individuals found <u>and</u> optimal or good habitat available.

> Declining (D) trend (i.e., longterm persistence is tenuous) is assigned if: (1) thorough post-1980 surveys failed to collect at least one specimen; **or** (2) post 1980 survey lacking <u>and</u> only a limited number of specimens collected during the previous survey, <u>and</u> habitat is very restricted; **or** (3) only mature <u>or</u> dead individuals found despite thorough surveys conducted over several years.

Presumed Declining (PD) trend (i.e., existing data suggests that longterm persistence is in doubt) is assigned if: (1) post 1980 collections of specimens (including juveniles and young adults) and habitat is very restricted; **or** (2) post 1980 surveys lacking and previous collections consist of only a few and optimal or good habitat is available.

Unknown (UK) trend is assigned if: (1) individuals have been collected since 1980 and no other information is available; **or** (2) post 1980 surveys lacking and habitat quality and quantity unknown.

Table 1: Alternate Format for Trend Categories for Extant Populations and Those of Uncertain Status

		Survey and Results				
		Post 1980; Juveniles or young adults collected	Post-1980; mature live or fresh dead found	Pre-1980 only; Few individ. collected previously	Thorough & post-1980; no live or fresh dead shells found	Post 1980, thorough surveys spanning sev.yrs; mature or fd shells only
Habitat Quality and Abundance	Optimal	S(no threats)	LS(2)	PD(3)	D(1)	D(3)
	Good	LS(1)	LS(2)	PD(3)	D(1)	D(3)
	Vy. Restricted	PD(1)	PD(1)	D(2)	D(1)	D(3)
	Unknown	UK	UK	UK	D(1)	D(3)

Table 2: *Leptodea leptodon* population status and trend.

River Population	Last Date Collected*[1]	Status *	Trend *	Threats **
UPPER MISSISSIPPI				
Mississippi River proper (IL, IA, WI)	pre-1958	X	NA	NA
Minnesota River (MN)	1800s	X	NA	NA
Burdett's(?Binde tte) Slough (IA)	1890	X	NA	NA
Iowa River (IA)	pre-1944	X	NA	NA
Cedar River (IA)	1882	X	NA	NA
Illinois River (IL)	pre-1887	X	NA	NA
Sangamon River (IL)	pre-1944	X	NA	NA
Pecatonica River (IL)	pre-1944	X	NA	NA
MIDDLE MISSISSIPPI				
Kaskaskia River (IL)	1921	X	NA	NA
Ohio River Proper (KY, OH)	1897	X	NA	NA
Wabash River (IL, IN)	pre-1919	X	NA	NA
White River (IN)	pre-1919	X	NA	NA
Sugar Creek (IN)	1925	X	NA	NA
Green River (KY)	1964	X	NA	NA
Licking River (KY)	pre-1950	X	NA	NA
Scioto River (OH)	1838	X	NA	NA

Table 2: *Leptodea leptodon* population status and trend.

River Population	Last Date Collected*[1]	Status *	Trend *	Threats **
St. Mary's River (OH)	1930	X	NA	NA
E. Fork Lt. Miami River (OH)	~1900	X	NA	NA
Cumberland River (KY, TN)	1964	X	NA	NA
Beaver Creek (KY)	1948	X	NA	NA
Caney Fork (TN)	pre-1950	X	NA	NA
Tennessee River (AL,TN)	pre-1950	X	NA	NA
Clinch River (TN)	pre-1950	X	NA	NA
Holston River (TN)	pre-1950	X	NA	NA
Duck River (TN)	pre-1950	X	NA	NA
Meramec River (MO)	1997	E	LS	
Big River (MO)	1997	E	PD	small pop., isolated and restricted habitat
Bourbeuse River (MO)	1997	E	LS	Small population
Auxvasse Creek (MO)	late 1960s	X	NA	
South Grand (MO)	early 1970s	X	NA	NA
Missouri River Proper (SD)	1983	X	NA	NA
Gasconade River (MO)	1994	E	PD	Sedimentation, Small population
Big Piney River (MO)	1981	UK	UK	

Table 2: *Leptodea leptodon* population status and trend.

River Population	Last Date Collected*[1]	Status *	Trend *	Threats **
LOWER MISSISSIPPI				
St. Francis River (AR)	1985	E	D	Limited habitat, Small population, Sedimentation
White River (AR)	1902	X	NA	NA
James River (AR)	pre-1950	X	NA	NA
Spring River (AR)	1991	E	PD	In-stream mining, Sedimentation, Nonpoint source pollution
S. Fork Spring (AR)	1990	E	LS	Unknown
Myatt Creek (AR)	1996	LX	UK	Unknown, Suspect small population if present
Strawberry River (AR)	1996	E	UK	Unknown, Suspect small population
Middle Fork Lt. Red River (AR)	1967	X	NA	NA
Poteau River (OK)	pre-1980	X	NA	NA
Frog Bayou (AR)	1979	LX	PD	Reservoirs, In-stream mining, Sedimentation
S. Fourche LaFave River (AR)	1991	E	PD	Limited habitat, Small population
Kiamichi River (OK)	1987	E	D	Small population, Proposed reservoir
Gates Creek (OK)	pre-1971	LX	PD	
Little River (OK)	1960	LX	D	Reservoir Impacts

Table 2: *Leptodea leptodon* population status and trend.

River Population	Last Date Collected*[1]	Status *	Trend *	Threats **
Mountain Fork (OK)	pre-1971	LX	D	Reservoir-potential, Suspect small population
Cossatot River (AR)	1983	E	UK	Small population
Saline River (AR)	1987	E	UK	Small population
Ouachita River (AR)	Old museum record	X	NA	NA
Lt. Missouri River (AR)	1995	E	UK	Suspect small population
Saline River, Ouachita Trib. (AR)	1946	X	NA	NA

*See Note on appendix page

**See text for citation and further discussion.

[1] Citation for Date Last Collected are as follows: **Illinois Natural History Survey** records (Mississippi River, Burdett's Slough, Sanagamon River, Illinois River, Kaskaskia River, Pecatonia River, Wabash River, White River, Sugar Creek, and Kiamichi River); **Clarke 1995** (St. Francis River); **Clarke 1996** (Cedar River, Big Piney River, Meramec River, Big River, E. Fork Lt. Miami River, Licking River, Beaver Creek, Caney Fork, Tennessee River, Clinch River, Holston River, Duck River, White River, Middle Fork Lt. Red River, AR, James River, Little River, Ouachita River, and Saline River); **Hoke 1983** (Missouri River); **Buchanan 1994** (Gasconade River); **Alan Buchanan**, Missouri Dept. of Nat. Res., *in litt.* 1997 (South Grand River and Auxvasse Creek); Buchanan 1980 (Bourbeus River); **Patricia Jones**, Ohio Dept. of Nat. Res., *in litt.* 1994 (Ohio River, Scioto River, and St. Mary's River); **Wayne Davis**, Kentucky Dept. of Fish and Game, pers. comm. 1994 (Green River, Beaver Creek, and Cumberland River); **John Harris**, Arkansas State, pers. comm. 1995, and *in litt.* 1996, 1997 (Spring River, S. Fork Spring, Myatt Creek, Strawberry River, Casatot River, Lt. Missouri River, and Saline River); **Harris 1992** (S. Forche Larve River); **Valentine and Stansbery 1971** (Gates Creek and Mountain Fork); **Gordon 1980** (Frog Bayou); **Gordon 1991** (Mulberry River and Poteau River)

Table 2: *Leptodea leptodon* population status and trend.

Table 2: *Leptodea leptodon* population status and trend.

RIVER DRAINAGE	DRAINAGE SUBDIVISION	RIVER SUBDIVISION	TRIBUTARY	STATE	
Upper Mississippi River					
	Mississippi River proper			IA,IL	Carroll (IL) (IA), Clayto
	Minnesota River			MN	Dakota
	Burdett's Slough			IA	Muscatine
	Iowa River	Iowa proper		IA	Johnson
		Cedar River		IA	Linn
	Illinois River	Illinois River		IL	Peoria
		Sanagamon River		IL	Menard
		Pecatonica River		IL	Stephenson
Middle Mississippi River					
	Kaskaskia River			IL	Washington
	Ohio River	Ohio River proper		KY,OH	Boone (KY Washington
		Wabash River proper		IL,IN	Posey (IN), Carroll (IN)
			White River	IN	Marian
			Sugar Creek	IN	Parke
		Green River		KY	Hart
		Licking River		KY	unknown
		Scioto River		OH	unknown
		St. Mary's River		OH	unknown
		E. Fork Lt. Miami River		OH	unknown

Table 2: *Leptodea leptodon* population status and trend.

RIVER DRAINAGE	DRAINAGE SUBDIVISION	RIVER SUBDIVISION	TRIBUTARY	STATE	
		Cumberland River proper		KY,TN, AL	Cumberland Colbert (AL
			Beaver Creek	KY	Russell
			Caney Fork	TN	Smith
		Tennessee River proper		AL,TN	Colbert (AL
			Clinch River	TN	Anderson
			Holston River	TN	Knox
			Duck River	TN	Unknown
	Meramec River	Meramec River proper		MO	Crawford, J
		Big River		MO	Jefferson
		Bourbeus River		MO	St. Louis, Je
	Missouri River	Missouri River Proper		SD	Yankton
		Gasconade River		MO	Gasconade,
			Big Piney River	MO	Pulaski
		South Grand		MO	Benton
		Auxvasse Creek		MO	Callaway
Lower Mississippi					
	St. Francis River	St. Francis proper		AR	St. Francis,
	White River	White River proper		AR	Benton
			James River	AR	Stone
		Spring River proper		AR	Sharpe, Ran
			S. Fork Spring	AR	Fulton

RIVER DRAINAGE	DRAINAGE SUBDIVISION	RIVER SUBDIVISION	TRIBUTARY	STATE	
			Myatt Creek	AR	Fulton
			Strawberry River	AR	Lawrence
		Middle Fork Lt. Red River		AR	Van Buren
	Arkansas River				
		Mulberry River		AR	Unknown
		Frog Bayou		AR	Sevier
		Poteau River		OK	LeFlore
		South Fourche LaFave River		AR	Perry
	Red River				
		Kiamichi River		OK	Choctaw, Pɪ
			Gates Creek	OK	Pushmataha
		Little River		OK	McCurtain
			Mountain Fork	OK	McCurtain
			Casatot River	AR	Sevier
			Saline River	AR	Sevier, Hov
		Ouachita River		AR	Clark
			Lt. Missouri River	AR	Clark
			Saline River	AR	Cleveland

* The exact locations of *Leptodea leptodon* collections was not given (Clarke 1985).

Table 4: State Legal Status and Population Trend

STATE	STATE LEGAL STATUS	POPULATION STATUS
Alabama	None (Extirpated[1])	Extirpated
Arkansas	None (Threatened[1])	Extant
Illinois	Extirpated	Extirpated
Indiana	Extirpated	Extirpated

Iowa	Extirpated	Extirpated
Kentucky	Extirpated	Extirpated
Minnesota	None (Extirpated)	Extirpated
Missouri	Rare[2]	Extant
Ohio	Extirpated	Extirpated
Oklahoma	Species of Concern	Extant
South Dakota	None	Extirpated
Tennessee	Extirpated	Extirpated
Wisconsin	Extirpated	Extirpated

[1]Species experts' unofficial designation
[2] State considering elevating to endangered status (Sue Bruenderman, Missouri DOC, pers. comm. 1998).

LITERATURE CITED

Ahlstedt, S.A. and J.J. Jenkinson. 1987. Distribution and abundance of *Potamilus capax* and other freshwater mussels in the St. Francis River System, Arkansas and Missouri. Unpublished Report prepared for U.S. Army Corps of Engineers, Memphis District, Contract No. PD-86-C052.

Arey, L.B. 1921. An experimental study on glochidia and the factors underlying encystment. J. Exp. Zool. 33:463-499.

Arkansas State Highway & Transportation Department. 1984. Relocation of the Pink Mucket Pearly Mussel (*Lampsilis orbiculata*) in the Spring River near Ravenden, Lawwrence County, Arkansas. 9p.

Baker, F.C. 1928. The fresh-water Mollusca of Wisconsin. Part II: Pelecypoda. University of Wisconsin Bulletin No. 70. 495p.

Bates, J.M. 1962. Impact of impoundment on the mussel fauna of Kentucky Reservoir, Tennessee River. American Midland Naturalist 68:232-236.

_____. and S.D. Dennis. 1983. Mussel (naiad) survey--St. Francis, White, and Cache rivers Arkansas and Missouri. Final Report prepared for U.S. Army Corps of Engineers, Memphis District, Contract No. DACW66-78-C-0147. 89 pp + appendices.

Bayne, B.L., K.R. Clarke, and M.N. Moore. 1981. Some practical considerations in the measurement of pollution effects on bivalve molluscs, and some possible ecological consequences. Aquat. Toxicol. 1:159-174.

Branson, B.A. 1984. The mussels (*Unionaceae:Bivalvia*) of Oklahoma- Part 3: Lampsilini. Proceedings Oklahoma Academy of Science 64:20-36.

Buchanan, A.C. 1980. Mussels (Naiades) of the Meramec River basin. Missouri Department of Conservation. Aquatic Series 17. 76p.

_____. 1994. A survey of the freshwater mussels of the lower Gasconade River. Report for U.S. Army of Corps of Engineers, Kansas City District, 700 Federal Building, Kansas City, MO 64106.

Cairns, J., J.S. Crossman, K.L. Dickson, and E.E. Herricks. 1971. The recovery of damaged streams. Association of Southeastern Biologists Bulletin 18:79-106.

Call, R.E. 1900. A descriptive illustrated catalogue of the Mollusca of Indiana. Indiana Department of Geology and Natural Resources Annual Report 24:335-535.

Chesters, G. and L. Schierow. 1985. A primer on nonpoint pollution. Journal of Soil and Water Conservation 40(1):9-13.

Clarke, A.H. 1985. Mussel (naiad) study: St. Francis and White rivers Arkansas. Unpublished Report submitted to U.S. Army of Corps of Engineers, Memphis District, Contract No. 84M

1666R. 28p.

_____. 1987. Status survey of *Lampsilis streckeri* and *Arcidens wheeleri*. Final Report to U.S. Fish and Wildlife Service, Jackson Mississippi Field Office. 24p.

_____. 1995. Survey of the mussel beds in the lower Ohio River. U.S. Army Corps of Engineers, Louisville District, Kentucky. 123p.

_____. 1996. Results of a biological survey for *Leptodea leptodon* (Rafinewsque, 1820) in the Missouri River in Southeastern South Dakota. Unpublished Report prepared for U.S. Fish and Wildlife Service, South Dakota Field Office. 13 pp + appendices.

Coon, T.G., J.W. Eckblad, and P.M. Trygstad. 1977. Relative abundance and growth of mussels (Mollusca: Eulamellibranchia) in pools 8, 9, and 10 of the Mississippi River. Freshwater Biology 7:279-285.

Cummings, K.S., and C.A. Mayer. 1992. Field guide to freshwater mussels of the Midwest. Illinois Natural History Survey Manual 5. 194p.

Dance, K.W. 1981. Seasonal aspects of organic and inorganic matter in streams. Pages 69-95 *in* Perspectives in running water ecology. Williams, D.D. and M.A. Lock, eds. Plenum Press, New York.

Downing, J.A., Rochon, Y. & M. Perusse. 1993. Spatial aggregation, body size, and reproductive success in the freshwater mussel *Elliptio complanata*. Journal of the North American Benthological Society 12:148-156.

Ellis, M.M. 1929. The artificial propagation of freshwater mussels. Trans. American Fish. Soc. 59:217-223.

_____. 1936. Erosion silt as a factor in aquatic environments. Ecology 17(1):29-42.

Fuller, S.L.H. 1974. Clams and mussels (Mollusca: Bivalvia). Pages 215-273 *in* C.W. Hart and S.L.H. Fuller, eds. Pollution ecology of freshwater invertebrates. Academic Press, Inc., New York.

Goodrich, C. and H. Van Der Schalie. 1944. A revision of the Mollusca of Indiana. Am. Midl. Nat. 32:257-326.

Gordon, M.E. 1980. Recent Mollusca of Arkansas with annotations to systematics and zoogeography. Proceedings Arkansas Academy of Science 34:58-62.

_____. 1984. Mussel Fauna of the Black and Spring rivers in northeastern Arkansas. Prepared for U.S. Army Corps of Engineers, Little Rock District. 27p.

_____. 1991. Species accounts for Cumberland elktoe (*Alasmidonta atropurpurea*), Cumberlandian combshell (*Epioblasma brevidens*), oyster mussel (*Epioblasma capsaeformis*), rough rabbitsfoot (*Quadrula cylindrica strigillata*), and purple bean (*Villosa perpurpurea*).

Unpublished report to The Nature Conservancy. 75p.

_____., L.R. Kraemer, and A.V. Brown. 1979. Unionidae of Arkansas, historical review, checklist and observations on distributional pattern. Bulletin of the American Malacological Union 1979:31-37.

_____. and J.B. Layzer. 1989. Mussels (Bivalvia: Unionoidea) of the Cumberland River: review of life histories and ecological relationships. U.S. Fish Wildlife Service Biol. Rep. 89(15). 99p.

_____., P.A. Durkee, H.M. Runke, and H.J. Zimmerman. 1984. Mussel fauna of the Black and Spring Rivers in northeastern Arkansas. Unpublished report prepared for Army Corps of Engineers, Little Rock District. 27p.

Goudreau, S.E., R.J. Neves, and R.J. Sheehan. 1988. Effects of sewage treatment plant effluents on mollusks and fish of the Clinch River in Tazewell County, Virginia. Final Report prepared for U.S. Fish and Wildlife Service, Asheville, North Carolina. 127p.

Harris, J.L. 1986. Relocation of the fat pocketbook pearly mussel, *Proptera capax,* in the St. Francis River at Madison, St. Francis County, Arkansas. Arkansas Highway and Transportation Department and Arkansas Game and Fish Comm., Little rock. 14p.

_____. 1992. Survey of the freshwater mussels (Mollusca: Unionidae) of the South Fourche LaFave River and major tributaries. Unpublish manuscript. 19 pp + appendices.

_____. 1994. Survey of the freshwater mussels (Mollusca: Unionidae) of the Poteau River drainage in Arkansas. Unpublished manuscript. 23 pp + appendices.

Harris, J.L. and M.E. Gordon. 1987. Distribution and status of rare and endangered mussels (Mollusca:Margaritiferidae, Unionidae) in Arkansas. Proceedings Arkansas Academy of Science 41:49-56.

Hartfield, P. 1993. Headcuts and their effect on freshwater mussels. Pages 131-141 *in* K.S. Cummings, A.C. Buchanan, and L.M. Koch (eds.), Conservation and management of freshwater musssels. Proceedings of a UMRCC symposium, 12-14 October 1992, St. Louis, Missouri. Upper Mississippi River Conservation Committee, Rock Island, Illinois.

Hoke, Ellet. 1983. Unionid mollusks of the Missouri River on the Nebraska border. Am. Mal. Bull., Vol. 1(1983):71-74.

Holwerda, D.A. and P.R. Veenhof. 1984. Aspects of anaerobic metabolism in *Anodonta cygnea l.* Comp. Biochem. Physiol B. 78:707-711.

Imlay, M.J. 1972. Greater adaptability of freshwater mussels to natural rather than to artificial displacement. The Nautilus 86(2-4):76-79.

_____. 1982. Use of Shells of freshwater mussels in monitoring heavy metals and environmental stresses: A Review. Malacological Review 15:1-14.

_____. and Paige, M.J. 1972. Laboratory growth of freshwater sponges, unionid mussels, and sphaeriid clams. The Progressive Fish-Culturist 34(4):210-216.

Isley, F. B. 1925. The fresh-water mussel fauna of eastern Oklahoma. Proceedings of the Oklahoma Academy of Science 4:43-118.

Jansen, W.A. and J.M. Hanson. 1991. Estimates of the number of glochidia produced by clams (*Anodonta grandis simpsonianus* Lea), attaching to yellow perch (*Perca flavescens*), and surviving to various ages in Narrow Lake, Alberta. Canadian Journal of Zoology 69:973-977.

Layzer, J.B., M.E. Gordon, and R.M. Anderson. 1993. Mussels: The forgotten fauna of regulated rivers. A case study of the Caney Fork River. Research & Management 8:63-71.

Lewis, J. 1868. Remarks on the mollusks of the Valley of the Mohawk. American Journal of Conchology 4:241-245.

Master, L. 1990. The imperiled status of North American aquatic animals. Biodiversity Network News 3:1-2, 7-8.

Matteson, M.R. 1948. Life history of *Elliptio complanatus*. American Midland Naturalist 40:690-723.

_____. 1955. Studies on the natural history of the Unionidae. American Midland Naturalist 53:126-145.

Miller, A.C. and D.A. Nelson. 1984. A Survey for mussels on the Black and Spring rivers, Arkansas, 17-19 November 1983. U.S. Army Engineer Waterways Experiment Station, Vicksburg, Mississippi. 10p.

_____. and P.D. Hartfield. 1986. A Survey for live mussels in the Black and Spring rivers, Arkansas, 1985. Prepared for U.S. Army Engineer, Little Rock District. 13 pp + appendicies.

Myers, C.F., J. Meek, S. Tuller, and A. Weinberg. 1985. Nonpoint sources of water pollution. Journal of Soil and Water Conservation 40(1):14-18.

Negus, C.L. 1966. A quantitative study of growth and production of unionid mussels in the river Thames at Reading. Journal of wildlife Management 53:934-941.

Neves, R.J. 1993. A state-of-the-unionids address. Pages 1-10 *in* K.S. Cummings, A.C. Buchanan, and L.M. Koch (eds.), Conservation and management of freshwater mussels. Proceedings of a UMRCC symposium, 12-14 October 1992, St.Louis, Missouri. Uper Mississipi River Conservation Committee, Rock Island, Illinois.

_____. 1994. Brooding over mussels. Virginia Wildlife. January (1994):4-9.

Noss, F.R. and A.Y. Cooperrider. 1994. Savings nature's legacy: Protecting and restoring biodiversity. Island Press, Washington D.C. 416p.

Oesch, R.D. 1984. Missouri naiades: A guide to the mussels of Missouri. Missouri Department of Conservation, Jefferson City, Missouri. 270p.

Ortmann, A.E. 1909. The destruction of the freshwater fauna in western Pennsylvania. Proceedings of the american Philopsophical Society 48(1):90-110.

Ray, R. H. 1977. Application of an acetate peal technique to analysis of growth processes in bivalve unionid shells. Bull. Am. malacolo. Union 44:79-82.

Rosenberg, G.D. and M.T. Henschen. 1986. Sediment particles as a cause of nacre staining in the freshwater mussel, *Ambema plicata* (Say) (Bivalvia: Unionidae). Hydrobiologia 135:167-178.

Sorensen, D.L., M.M. McCarthy, E.J. Middlebrooks, and D.B. Porcella. 1977. Suspended and dissolved solids effects on freshwater biota: A review. Corvallis Environmenntal Research Laboratory. 65 p.

Spacie, A., and A.M. Chaney. 1993. Metabloic effects of suspended solids on unionid mussels. Unpublished report submitted to Indiana Department of Natural Resources, Indianapolis, Indiana. 52 p + apendices.

Stansbery, A.H. 1976. Naiad mollusks. Bull. Alabama Museum Nat. Hist. (2):42-52.

Stoeckel, J.N., L. Lewis, and S. Shook. 1995. Mulberry River Freshwater mussel survey. Unpublished manuscript. 6 p.

Tessier, A., and P.G.C. Campbell. 1987. Partitioning of trace metals in sediments: Relationships with bioavailability. Hydrobiologia 28:707-714.

Thomas, L.M. 1985. Viewpoint: Management of nonpoint-source pollution: What priority? Journal of Soil and Water Conservation 40(1):8

U.S. Environmental Protection Agency (USEPA). 1990. The quality of our nation's water: a summary of the 1988 National Water Quality Inventory. U.S. Environmental Protection Agency, EPA Report 440/4-90-005, Washington D.C.

U.S. Fish and Wildlife Service (USFWS). (In prep.) Technical/Agency Draft, Revised Recovery Plan for Higgins' Eye Pearly Mussel. Ft. Snelling, MN.

U.S. Soil Conservation Service (USSCS). 1988. Water quality field guide. United States Department of Agriculture. 63 p.

Valentine, B.D. and D. H. Stansbery. 1971. An introduction to the naiads of the Lake Texoma region, Oklahoma, with notes on the Red River fauna (Mollusca: Unionidae). Sterkiana. 42:1-25.

Vaughn, C.C. 1993. Can biogeographic models be used to predict the persistence of mussel popualtions in rivers? Pages 117-122 *in* K.S. Cummings, A.C. Buchanan, and L.M. Koch (eds.), Conservation and management of freshwater musssels. Proceedings of a UMRCC symposium, 12-14 October 1992, St. Louis, Missouri. Uper Mississipi River Conservation Committee, Rock

Island, Illinois.

_____. 1994. Survey for *Arkansia wheeleri* in the Little River. Final report submitted to U.S. Fish and Wildlife Service, Tulsa, Oklahoma. 23 pp + map.

Waters, T.F. 1995. Sediment in streams: Sources, biological effects, and control. American Fisheries Society Monograph 7.

Watters, T.J. 1995. A guide to the freshwater mussels of Ohio, third ed. Published by the Ohio Division of Wildlife, Columbus, Ohio. 122p.

White, D.S. 1977. Changes in the freshwater mussel populations of the Poteau River system, LeFlore County, Oklahoma. Proceedings Oklahoma Academy of Science. 57:103-105.

Wilson, C.B., and H.W. Clark. 1912. The mussel fauna of the Kankakee basin. Rep. U.S. Comm. Fish. for 1911 and Spec. Papers, p. 1-52. Separately issued as Bur. Fish. Document No. 758.

Williams, J.D., M.L. Warren, K.S. Cummings, J.L. Harris, and R.J. Neves. 1993. Conservation status of freshwater mussels of the United States and Canada. Fisheries 18(9):6-22.

Wolcott, L.T. and R.J. Neves. 1990. Impacts of siltation on the mussel fauna of the Powell River, Virginia. Final report submitted to U.S. Fish and Wildlife Service, Asheville, North Carolina. 115p.

Young, D. 1911. The implantation of the glochidium on the fish. University of Missouri Bulletin Science Series 2:1-20.

Young, M. and J. Williams. 1984. The reproductive biology of the freshwater pearl mussel *Margaritifera margaritifiera* (Linn.) in Scotland. I. Field studies. Archiv fur Hydrobiologie 99:405-422.

CONTACT LIST

Steve Ahlstedt (1995)
Tennessee Valley Authority,
Aquatic Biology Dept., P.O. Box 460
Norris, TN 37828   615/494-9800

Bob Anderson
U.S. Geological Survey
1000 Liberty Ave. Rm. 2204
Pittsburg, PA 15222   412/644-2278

Gerry Bade
U.S. Fish and Wildlife Service
Rock Island Field Office
4469 48th Ave. Ct.
Rock Island, IL 61201   309/793-5800

Richard Baker
Endangered Resource Specialist
Dept. of Nat. Resources
500 Lafayette Road
St. Paul, MN 55155-40   612/297-3764

Terry Balding
UW-Eau Claire
Dept. of Biology,
Eau Claire, WI 54702-4004   715/836-4415

Richard Biggins
U.S. Fish and Wildlife Service
Asheville Field Office
160 Zillicoa Street
Asheville, NC 28806   704/258-3939ext. 228.

Arthur Bogan
Freshwater Molluscan Research
36 Venus Way
Sewell, NJ 08080-1970   609/582-9113

Sue Bruenderman
Missouri Dept. of Conservation.
Fish and Wildlife Research Center
1110 College Ave.
Columbia, MO 65201   573/882-9880ext. 3239

Allan Buchanan
Missouri dept. of Conservaiton
Fish and Wildlife Research Center
1110 College Ave.
Columbia, MO 65201   573/882-9880

Cindy Chaffee
U.S. Fish and Wildlife Service
Olympia Washington Field Office
510 Desmond Dr. SE, Suite 102

	Lacey, WA 98503	360/753-4324
Ron Cicerello	Kentucky Nature Preserves Commission 407 Broadway Frankfort, KY 40601	502/564-2886
Arthur Clarke	Ecosearch, Inc. 325 E. Bayview Ave. Portland, TX 78374	512/643-6613
Kevin Cummings	Illinois Natural History Survey 607 Peabody Dr. Champaign, IL 61820	217/333-1623
Mike Davis	Minnesota Dept. of Natural Resources Mississippi River Office R.R. 2 Box 230 Lake City, MN 55041	612/345-331
Wayne Davis	Kentucky Dept. of Fish and Game Resources 1 Game Farm Road Frankfort, KY 40601	502/564-5448
Heidi Dunn	Ecological Specialists 114 Algana Court St. Peters, MO 63376	314/447-5355
Jeff Garner	Alabama Dept. of Conservation & Natural Resources P.O. Box 366 Decatur, AL 35602	205/353-2634
Jim Godwin	Alabama Natural Heritage Program Dept. of Conservation & Natural Resources 64 N Union St., Rm 752 Montgomery, AL 36130	
John Harris	Arkansas State University 12301 Pleasant Forest Drive Little Rock, AR 72212	501/569-2281
Paul Hartfield	U.S. Fish and Wildlife Service 6578 Dogwood View Parkway Jackson , Mississippi 39213	601/965-4900 ext. 25
Marian Havlik	Malacological Consultants 1603 Mississippi St. La Crosse, WI 54601	608/782-7958

David Heath	Wisconsin Dept. of Natural Resources Box 818 Rhinelander, WI 54501 715/362-7616
Craig Hilborn	U.S. Forest Service- St. Francis District
Michael Hoggarth	Otterbein College Dept. of Life & Earth Sciences Westerville, OH 43081
Daryll Howell	Iowa Dept. of Natural Resources Bureau Preserves and Ecology, Henry Wallace Bldg. Des Moines, IA 50319 515/281-8524
John Jenkinson	Tennessee Valley Authority Aquatic Biology Dept., Water Resources 1101 Market St., HB 2C Chattanooga, TN 37402 615/751-6903
Wally Jobman	U.S. Fish and Wildlife Service Nebraska Field Office 203 W. 2nd St., 2nd floor Grand Island, NE 68801 308/382-6468 ext. 16
Patricia Jones	Ohio Dept. of Natural Resources Div. of Natural Areas and Preserves 1889 Fountain Square Crt, Bldg. F, Columbus, OH 43224 614/265-6472
Paul MacKenzie	U.S. Fish and Wildlife Service Missouri Field Office 608 Cherry St. Rm 200 Columbia, Missouri 65201 314/876-1911
Stuart McGregor	Geological Survey of Alabama 420 Hackberry Lane, P.O. Box 0 Tuscaloosa, AL 35486-9780 205/349-2852
David Martinez	U.S. Fish and Wildlife Service 222 S. Houston Suite A Tulsa, OK 74125 918/581-7458 ext.228
Charles Mather	University of Science and Arts of Oklahoma Box 82517 Chickasha, OK 73018 405/224-7959

Nell McPhillips
U.S. Fish and Wildlife Service
South Dakota Field Office
420 S. Gardield Ave., Suite 400
Pierre, SD 57501-5408   605/224-8693

David Michaelson
U.S. Fish and Wildlife Service
Missouri Field Office
608 Cherry St. Rm 200
Columbia, Missouri 65201   314/876-1911

Drew Miller
U.S. Army Corps of Engineers
Waterways Experiment Station
Vicksburg, MS 39180   601/634-3111

Richard Neves
Virginia Polytechnic Institute and State University
Dept. of Fisheries and Wildlife Sciences
Balcksburg, VA 24061   703/231-5573

Ron Oesch
872 Fuhrmann Terrace
Allendale, MO 63122

Cindy Osborne
Arkansas Natural Hertiage Commisssion
1500 Tower Building, 323 Center St.
Little Rock, AR 72201   501/324-9618

Paul Parmelee
The University of Tennessee
Dept. of Anthropology
Knoxville, TN 37916

Allan Price
Arkansas Pollution and Ecology Dept.
P.O. Box 8913
Little Rock, AR 72219   501/682-0744

Tom Proch
Pennsylvania Dept. of Envoronmental Research
2721 Cedric Ave.
Pittsburgh, PA 15226

Andy Roberts
12672 A Mateus Dr.
St. Louis, MO 63146   314/514-9703

Lynn Scrimger
Michigan Natural Features Inventory
Dept. of Natural Resources
Stevens T Mason Building
P.O. Box 30444
Lansing, MI 48909-7944

Katie Smith

Indiana Dept. of Natural Resources
402 W. Washington St., Rm W273
Indianapolis, IN 46204

317/232-4080

David Stansbery

Ohio State University
Museum of Biological Diversity
1315 Kinnear Road
Columbus, Ohio 43212-1192

614/292-8560

Bill Tolin

U.S. Fish and Wildlife Service
West Virgina Field Office
P.O. Box 1278
Elkins, WV 26241

304/636-6586

Caryn Vaughn

Oklahoma Natural Heritage Inventory
111E. chesapeake Street
University of Oklahoma
Norman, OK, 73019-0543

405/325-2753

Thomas Watters

Ohio Dept. of Natural Resources
The Division of Wildlife
1840 Belcher Drive
Columbus, OH 43224-1329

614/292-6170

Bob Whiting

US Army Corps of Engineers
190 5th St. East
St. Paul, MN 55101-1638

612/290-5264.

Paul Yokley

University of North Alabama
Dept. of Biology
Florence, AL 35630